You had never seen before you began to see...

You had never heard before you began to hear...

You had never spoken before you began to speak...

You had never walked before you began to walk...

Whatever it is that you want to do,

begin...

and do so without any fear from not having done so yet.

For there was a time, that everything you have done,

was something you had never done before.

On The Way

Steven Adams

ISBN: 978-1-946022-22-6

First Printing, 2017

thedowntowncrown publishing group
New York, N.Y.

To Mom and Dad...

You taught me the two most valuable things anyone can learn in this life...to always be true to myself, and how to love with everything I've got. You never tried to put limits on my dreams or stop me from going down any road, that I knew in my heart, I needed to follow. For this I dedicate my life's work to you.

And...to all of those who've inspired me, in ways big and small. I thank you for your words, your actions, your presence. It is the courage and conviction you've shown in sharing your own stories and wisdom with me, that has shown me how to do the same.

Contents

Before We Begin...

Have you ever wondered…

…what it means to be happy?

…why it seems so many people consistently struggle with becoming and remaining happy?

…is there a way to consciously, intentionally and purposefully manifest and sustain happiness in our lives?

These are some of the questions that, along with my attempts at answering them, began to swirl around in my head and ultimately land on the pages that have become this book. At first, it was not my intention to even go about writing a book. However, rather than continuing to think incessantly and ultimately getting nowhere as per usual, I began writing my thoughts down as a way to more deeply reflect on what I was going through and hopefully come to some semblance of a meaningful conclusion. However, the more and more I thought, and the more and more I wrote, I couldn't help but conclude that if I was thinking and feeling these things, there had to be others who were thinking and feeling the exact same things too. If that was indeed the case, then others might benefit from my experience and all that I've learned as a result.

What you're holding in your hands right now is a dose of medicine that I'd been badly in need of,… and just maybe you are too. It's inexplicable how, in our greatest times of need, glimpses of wisdom are doled out by the universe in sudden, inspired bolts. This often seems to happen at the very moment that the answers to our most burning questions seem their most elusive. I'd venture to say that the ultimate goal of life for most people is to be happy. But what does that really mean, or even look like? Assuming we know what happiness is, how many of us are able to consciously, intentionally and purposefully manifest and sustain it? In the midst of a time of great tribulation, and out of sheer necessity, I committed to an attempt at making sense of it all. I resolved to finding a way to not only come to a deeper understanding of the true nature of happiness, but also learn how to manifest and sustain it, as well.

So, here goes everything...

I've been relentlessly ambitious for most of my life and have never been one to really be satisfied with settling for second best or second place. While this kind of mentality can drive you to achieve tremendous things, there is also a very ugly, insidious and often concealed flip side to this way of living. When you're incredibly driven and things don't go according to plan, it's very easy for frustration, disillusionment and exhaustion to creep up on you rather quickly. Once you find yourself bearing the load of these demons (and it can be hard to even notice that you are, at first), it can seem almost impossible to pull yourself out of the ensuing spiral. In the prolonged absence of the results you seek, you continue to push, and push harder, until you reach a breaking point. It's at such a crossroads that you either acquiesce to your circumstances, or find a way to let the experience help you grow. This is right about where I was when I began to write this book.

Considering the fact that I don't really know how to quit at anything, it didn't take long for the cracks to show when life seemed to stop giving me what I wanted, despite my best intentions and effort. After a series of what I'll call "almost-there's", in both my personal and professional lives, I started asking the all-encompassing existential question, "What's it all for?". After all of the blood, sweat and tears I'd expended, and having very little in the way of something to show for it, I couldn't help but feel quite lost. I had been rendered unable to make sense of my life and all that was, and was not, happening. It became glaringly obvious that something needed to change, and that something was me. To say anything other than that I'm truly blessed and incredibly fortunate would be a bold-faced lie. In so many ways my life looks like one you'd find attached to an overwhelmingly happy person, but I wasn't. I found myself terribly conflicted and couldn't help but think that I didn't deserve to feel this way, given all that I have. However, that did little to change the fact that I had become increasingly unhappy.

It was then that I began to wonder what I thought happiness even was, and question the ways in which I had been going about seeking it. What I realized was that I had been committing a fatal mistake by defining my happiness within the context of my thoughts and feelings, and making my happiness contingent on the manifestation of certain things in my life (whether in the form of acquiring material possessions or achieving specific outcomes). It became clear that this was the direct result of the way in which most of us have been conditioned by society. From a very early age, we are instructed to set goals, work hard and meet or exceed expectations by doing whatever it takes to achieve the desired result. What usually accompanies this is a completely absurd disregard for how we go about it and the effect it can have on our lives. We've been indoctrinated into an "ends justifies the means" mentality that seems to permeate almost every aspect of life. So long as we achieve the goal, that's all that matters. To make things worse, we've been conditioned to woefully undervalue and squander the present in exchange for something that might never actually manifest.

As a result, many of us have acquiesced to grinding it out, day after day, doing things that make us unhappy in the present, in hope that we'll potentially be rewarded for it at some point down the road. This seemed both utterly insane and intrinsically counterintuitive to how life should be lived. After all, who would ever agree to spending the majority of their life doing things that make them unhappy, for the mere chance at the occasional glimpse of happiness? The chase that has come to define modern living, comes at the highest of costs. When, why and how did happiness become the exception rather than the rule?

This realization led me to believe that not only do many of us not fully comprehend the true nature of happiness, but that we also don't know how to manifest and sustain it in our lives. Regardless of what each of us wants out of life, it can't be denied that most of our time is spent *On The Way* to whatever that is. It would then make perfect sense that we need to find a way to become and remain happy in the course of actually living our lives and not resign ourselves to a chronic state of dissatisfaction, or deliberately and unnecessarily postpone our happiness.

In the pages that follow, we will discuss not only the nature of true happiness and the reasons why so many struggle to actually become and remain happy, but also come to an understanding of how we can manifest and sustain happiness in a straightforward, meaningful and practical way. Ultimately, knowledge is of little value if we can't or don't use it. As such, this book was written with accessibility, practicality and economy firmly in mind. It's structured in a way to be more of an engaging and thought-provoking conversation with the reader, and less a set of instructions. That being said, there is an intentional, logical flow to the way the ideas in this book are presented that will hopefully help you more easily and more profoundly integrate this practice into your life.

It is my sincerest hope that the message in this book reaches all of those who need it as much as I did. May it resonate in such a way that all who read it are not only constructively challenged to re-evaluate how they define happiness, but ultimately become and remain truly happy.

On The Way

Have We Lost Our Way?

What would you say is the most important thing in life?

I bet most of us would answer that question with some variation of the notion of "happiness".

No matter what you do or don't, or what you have or haven't, none of it really matters unless you're happy, does it?

You could be surrounded by the best of everything life has to offer, and if you're not happy, none of it would really be worth all that much.

I think we can all agree that happiness is so vital, that without it, life has very little in the way of meaning.

So, if we can agree that happiness is the most important thing in life, it would naturally follow that we begin by asking whether or not we consider ourselves to actually be happy in the first place.

I think most of us would respond to that particular question with an answer that lies somewhere within the bell curve between "yes" and "no".

While most of us probably aren't miserable, I wouldn't necessarily say we are overwhelmingly and consistently happy, either.

So, even if your answer is closer to "yes" than "no", I'd venture to say that "yes" is closer to "sometimes" than "always".

It's rather odd then, (and even sadly ironic) that while most people probably consider happiness to be the most important thing in life, they aren't actually all that happy on a consistent basis and are at a true loss for how to live genuinely happy lives.

The common experience of what most of us have come to know as "happiness", is something inherently elusive and fleeting, at best. In the event that we're fortunate enough to seize a random moment of "happiness" (or perhaps even string a few of these moments together), somehow the feeling inevitably fades, only to be quickly replaced by the all-too-familiar undercurrent of dissatisfaction that has unfortunately become the status quo for many.

It would appear on the surface that happiness is something very much beyond our control and can only be experienced in a haphazard, or accidental way.

But no matter what our experience of happiness has been up to this point, would we really acquiesce to a life that is less than genuinely and sustainably happy if there was something we could actually do about it...?

I didn't think so.

And that is exactly why we're here, in this moment, with these words.

Thus, we arrive at the ultimate purpose for this book: to understand the nature of true happiness and find a way to consciously, intentionally and purposefully manifest and sustain it in our lives.

In good faith, I acknowledge the fact that a number of schools of thought on happiness and its pursuit abundantly exist. However, with the multitude of people who are still living lives that are less-than-happy, I can't help but think that even with the best of intentions, these other ideologies have serious inherent flaws in either philosophy or practice.

In my personal experience, the challenge with most philosophies has always seemed to be the absence of a viable way to practically apply them. We might be able to comprehend and agree with them on an intellectual level, but without a way to functionally integrate them into our lives, we are left with knowledge merely for the sake of itself.

In the pages that follow, what I hope to offer you is an approach that is logical to understand, practical to apply and substantive enough to actually give you the ability to manifest and sustain true happiness in your life.

So, let's revisit the original question..."Are you happy?", and assume that your answer lies in the grey area between "yes" and "no".

Given your answer, have you ever stopped to thoughtfully ask yourself why this might be the case? And if so, have you given yourself the enough time to arrive at a complete and honest answer? If not, hopefully you will take the opportunity to do so, here and now.

There are likely as many different answers to this question as there are people answering it. However, if we could categorize these responses into major themes, I'd say that some of the most common would include: lack of self-awareness, compromised self-image, insecurity, inability or unwillingness to be honest with yourself or others, lack of accountability, unhealthy relationship boundaries, incompatible belief systems and fear. While each of these might have varying degrees of presence and influence within our lives, they are ultimately secondary to the two most fundamental, and equally important, issues that cause people to struggle with manifesting and sustaining happiness.

The first fundamental issue is that most of us operate under a definition of happiness that is incredibly ambiguous and widely open to interpretation.

The second issue is that most of us are either not taught how to manifest and sustain happiness in our lives, or are improperly taught how to do so.

In short, not only do most people not know what happiness truly is, they have never actually been taught how to consciously and intentionally manifest or sustain it in their lives. Without a meaningful understanding of what happiness is or the knowledge to manifest and sustain it, we can easily see why so many of us struggle with becoming and remaining happy.

However, before we can move forward to learn how to go about actually manifesting and sustaining happiness in our lives, we must first address the two most significant obstacles blocking our path.

This brings us to the next logical question, "Do you actually know what happiness is?".

What's In A Name?

As we just stated, the first fundamental issue that prevents most of us from becoming and remaining happy is that we operate under a definition that is incredibly vague and widely open to interpretation. The reason why this is a such a significant obstacle to happiness is three-fold.

First, in the absence of a clear definition of happiness, it becomes inherently difficult to know exactly what we're seeking in the first place.

Second, in the absence of a clear definition of happiness, it's challenging to evaluate or measure our experience.

Third, in the absence of a clear definition of happiness, it becomes all-the-more likely that we fall prey to unhealthy and unrealistic conceptualizations of happiness and/or ways to go about seeking it.

If we begin with the textbook, dictionary definition, it's clear why many of us don't really have a solid understanding of what happiness is.

Happiness - n., a state of well-being or contentment

Well, that's not vague or non-descript (please note the sarcasm), right?!

Putting the dictionary aside, I think most of us would probably describe happiness as a thought or feeling.

However, this is not only inaccurate, it's also still quite ambiguous and ultimately unhelpful, as well.

So, the first logical step toward becoming and remaining happy is to more clearly define what we believe happiness actually is, and is not.

The definition of happiness I'd like to offer here is: a positive, powerful, consistent and durable state of being that can be manifested and sustained by the individual, at will.

An experience along the lines of this definition lies in stark contrast to what most of us have been conditioned to believe happiness actually is.

In fact, if we've been taught to seek anything, it's not happiness at all, but pleasure. As a society, we have been taught to equate pleasure with happiness.

As one half of the pleasure-pain duality, pleasure cannot exist without pain. As such, pleasure cannot be equated with happiness because although it has the potential to be powerful (though, not always the case) it can never be consistent or durable, as it will always and inevitably fade and give way to pain.

Pleasure is an externally-rooted experience and its nature confines it to the realms of thought and feeling (both emotional and physical). As our external environment (along with our internal environments of thought and feeling) are subject to unpredictable, uncontrollable and radical fluctuations, so is pleasure. Thus, it cannot be manifested and sustained by the individual, at will.

Upon close examination and contrast of the two, it's obvious that pleasure is inferior to happiness in every single respect.

Let's deconstruct the different elements of our definition of happiness in order to better understand why each is necessary to manifest and sustain a state of being that is positive, powerful, durable and consistent. We'll do this by elaborating on the meaning of each, and contrasting them against the inverse characteristics of pleasure.

Happiness is positive...it is solely a beneficial experience and is never accompanied by negative side effects.

As we noted earlier, pleasure operates as one half of the pleasure-pain duality and is intrinsically linked to the endless cycle of want and satisfaction. By attempting to source our happiness with pleasure, we inevitably find ourselves trapped in a chase after needs that are never fully met or satisfied. Every pleasurable experience paves the way for a painful one.

Happiness is powerful...it is, by nature, transcendent and transformative. Its presence is unmistakable and its effects undeniable. Happiness is an experience felt on the deepest levels of our being and profoundly impacts not only ourselves, but everything and everyone around us, as well.

Pleasure has the potential to be powerful, but can never truly be transcendent or transformative. As it exists solely in the realms of thought and feeling, it does not have the strength to change who we are on the most fundamental levels of being or have a tangible impact on the world or others. It is very much a self-contained experience.

Happiness is durable...it is resilient. Happiness exists independently of the influence of our external environment and the lower levels of thought and emotion within our internal environment. It remains unaltered, even in the face of life's most significant challenges. Happiness not only magnifies life's positive experiences, but also withstands life's challenging experiences, as well.

Pleasure can easily give way to pain even under the slightest amount of pressure or stress that we may encounter. As we said earlier, it is inherently elusive and fleeting, at best.

Happiness is consistent...it is steady and unwavering in intensity. It is an experience that is either fully-present or non-existent.

Pleasure's intensity can fluctuate and is not only unpredictable, but wildly inconsistent. As an experience, it can range from intense to barely noticeable.

Ultimately, true happiness exists at the deepest levels of being and consciousness. It is firmly and exclusively rooted within the self.

In contrast, pleasure is rooted in the external environment and the lower levels of thought and feeling that exist within our internal environment.

The fact that we have been taught or conditioned to find happiness in pleasure is exactly why most of us never end up becoming truly and consistently happy.

However, the problem lies not only in what we've been conditioned to believe happiness is, but also how we've been conditioned to go about seeking it.

Let's explore this further by discussing the reasons why the way we've been taught to go about seeking happiness has ultimately failed us.

What, Why & How?

As we stated earlier, the second fundamental issue that causes most of us to struggle with manifesting and sustaining happiness in our lives, is that we have either not actually been taught how, or have been taught how to go about this in a way that is fundamentally flawed.

So, let's begin, as we did in the previous section, with a question..."How do you go about manifesting and sustaining happiness in your life?". Or, perhaps we can ask the question another way, "What makes you happy?".

I'm fairly certain that most of the responses to that question would resemble things like "money", "a house", "a relationship", "winning a game", "landing a job", etc.

After all, how many times have we heard someone else or even ourselves say something like, "If only I had "X" I'd be happy", or "If only "Y" happened, I'd be happy".

I also bet that very few of the responses to that question would resemble things like "writing", "building something", "playing a sport", "singing", "running", etc.

Did you happen to notice the difference between these two sets of answers?

The first list is comprised of objects and outcomes, while the second list is comprised of behaviors.

The reason that the majority of responses to that question fall into the categories of objects and outcomes is that these are the things we have been taught will make us happy.

And therein lies the second fundamental issue that contributes to people's struggle with manifesting and sustaining happiness in their lives.

As we said earlier, we've been taught to seek pleasure, not happiness, and the way in which we've been taught to seek this false "happiness" is primarily through the acquisition of material possession and achievement of specific outcomes.

Let's look at this a little more closely to understand why attempting to find happiness in objects and outcomes is ultimately problematic.

First, any "happiness" that can be derived from the acquisition of objects and the achievement of outcomes is not entirely within our control.

While objects and outcomes may be within our sphere of influence to some degree, they are not within our complete control. As such, any "happiness" that can be derived from objects and outcomes is also not within our complete control. It is paramount to become conscious of, and completely accept the fact that, almost everything in our lives is outside of our complete control. This includes the physical world around us...the thoughts, feelings and behaviors of others,...and even some of our own thoughts and feelings. Making our happiness contingent on such unreliable things leaves it to nothing more than chance, and, in the end, inevitably results in our disappointment.

Second, any "happiness" that can be derived from the acquisition of objects and the achievement of outcomes is time-bound and future tense.

By making our happiness dependent on things or events that may or may not manifest in the future, we are not only denying ourselves the possibility of happiness in the present moment, but we again leave our happiness to mere chance. As we are not guaranteed anything but this very moment, making our happiness dependent on anything in the future renders it fundamentally uncertain.

Third, any "happiness" that can be derived from the acquisition of objects and the achievement of outcomes is inherently self-limiting.

Most of us are taught, from a very young age, to set goals and become fixated on the pursuit of very specific things. By doing so, we can become so attached to definitive and inflexible visions of how we'd like our lives to unfold, that we fail to see other options that would make us happier. We also usually end up considering ourselves to be failures when life doesn't align explicitly to our expectations.

Fourth, any "happiness" that can be derived from the acquisition of objects and the achievement of outcomes is usually very short-lived.

Have you ever noticed that whatever "happiness" that might result after getting something we really want, no matter how badly or how long we've wanted it, tends to fade rather quickly after we get it? And what happens next? We begin to look for the next thing and the next thing, and so on... we basically end up becoming insatiable pleasure addicts, chasing the next high along a road that will never take us in the direction of true happiness.

Ultimately, most of us live our lives from the outside in, as opposed to the inside out. We allow our happiness to be dictated primarily by our external environments and experience. By living this way, everything seems to be happening to us, rather than having the ability to consciously manifest our lives and our happiness in an intentional and purposeful way. We are ultimately rendered victims of our own circumstance and our experience of happiness becomes unpredictable and unreliable. Thus, we can conclude that there is no real way for us to manifest and sustain true happiness by hinging it on the acquisition of objects and the achievement of outcomes.

But, if seeking happiness in this manner is not the answer, then what is?

Well, in the context of our human experience, there is but one thing that is not only within our complete control, but requires presence and supports a state of being that is powerful, durable, consistent and sustainable...can you guess what that might be?

Wait for it...wait for it...

As you may have guessed...

Behaviors

Behaviors

Behaviors

Let's continue by exploring the reasons why focusing on our behaviors is the only way that we can actually manifest and sustain true happiness.

What's Your Verb?

So why exactly are behaviors the key to becoming and remaining happy?

First, beyond everything else in life, our behaviors are the only aspect of our lives that we have complete control over.

As we discussed earlier, everything around us in the physical world...the thoughts, feelings and behaviors of others...and even some of our own thoughts and feelings (while potentially within our sphere of influence) are never completely within our control. If we therefore want to manifest and sustain a happiness that is positive, powerful, durable and consistent, wouldn't it make sense to source that with the only thing we have complete control over?

Second, engaging in any behavior is always a present-tense experience.

You are either doing something or not doing something in this moment. Engaging in behaviors is inherently something that belongs exclusively to the present. It would then naturally follow that the happiness derived from engaging in behaviors is manifested in the present, as well. There is no uncertainty or time delay that is experienced as would be the case by hinging our happiness on objects and outcomes.

Third, when we engage in behaviors solely for the sake of engaging in them, without regard for whatever might be gained or achieved as a result, we allow an endless number of possibilities to manifest.

Just as we noted that narrowly focusing on the acquisition and achievement of specific objects and outcomes could potentially limit us and our happiness, engaging in a behavior for the pure love of doing it, allows our lives the possibility of limitless expression. Ultimately, we never know what's going to happen next in our lives, regardless of whether or not we have a very clear and fixed vision of that we want that to be. However, focusing on engaging in something that supports our happiness in the present moment allows us to see uncertainty as possibility, and not something to fear.

Fourth, the happiness manifested by behaviors is sustainable.

The reason for this is that it's entirely up to us what behaviors we want to engage in, as well as when to engage in them. While taking this approach shifts the responsibility for manifesting and sustaining happiness onto the individual, this should be ultimately empowering. We no longer have to subject our happiness to the whim of everything and everyone else around us. Through shifting our focus toward behaviors and away from acquisition and achievement, we become consciously aware of the reality that manifesting and sustaining our happiness is entirely up to us. We are no longer rendered victims of circumstance, but become masters of our lives and our happiness.

Fifth, sourcing our happiness with our behaviors is the bridge between the ideological and the practical.

As we discussed at the beginning of the book, many of the other ideologies and teachings that are focused on happiness are not particularly applicable in a practical, everyday manner. Even something as fairly common and widely-practiced as meditation, while reasonably effective in the moment, is limited by the fact that we can't sit around and meditate all day. Now, don't misunderstand me. I consider meditation to be an undeniable and beautiful practice, but not everyone does. Some engage in it in a way that relegates it to more of a necessary evil than something loved. Yet others use it as a way of escaping reality, as opposed to fully embracing it. However, why wouldn't we just construct our lives in such a way such that we don't need to break away from them? By sourcing our happiness with our behaviors, we can actually transform our lives into an active, living meditation. In a way, we transpose the basic principles of yoga from the classroom into the entirety of our life experience.

Now that we know that the only way to truly manifest and sustain genuine happiness in our lives is by focusing on our behaviors, how do we go about actually doing this?

We need to begin by taking a closer and deeper look at how we're currently living our lives and what our idea of happiness presently looks like. Is it focused on objects and outcomes, or is it focused behaviors?

Self-examination and the heightened awareness that blooms from it aren't necessarily easy for most of us. It's difficult to look at our own lives with an objective eye and be honest and critical enough to recognize things we might need to change as well as take the necessary action to initiate that change.

And there is the big "c" word, "change", which is something that can seem almost impossible for many. After all, if the laws of physics apply to the universe around us, they apply just as easily to our lives, as well. The First Law of Motion states that an object will remain at rest, or in uniform motion in a straight line, unless compelled to change its state by influence of an external force. Such is the case for many of us and the reason behind our resistance to change. We tend to continue living life the same way that we always have, and doing the same things over and over, even if we become increasingly unhappy. It usually takes a significant adverse external event for many of to be motivated to initiate real change in our lives.

Focusing our attention on our behaviors, while perhaps not initially easy, is a necessary shift to break out of the conditioned cycle of pleasure and pain.

As we said, we need to take an honest and critical look at how we're living our lives right now and the ways in which we're currently seeking happiness,...so let's get to it.

A few sections ago we asked the question, "What would make you happy?". Well, let's ask that again, and this time, let's actually spend some time trying to figure out exactly what that is.

As part of this process, I encourage you to write down a list of everything that you believe currently makes you happy. Even though you now know that the answer to manifesting and sustaining happiness is behaviors, don't cheat. Be very honest with your list. If you're not, you'll just be sabotaging yourself and unable to reap the profound benefits of this practice. Take your time and really think this through. This is a crucial starting point of the process through which we'll learn how to manifest and sustain happiness.

Well, what did you discover? How much of your happiness is dependent upon objects and outcomes and how much upon behaviors?

Hopefully after going through this exercise, you'll have become much more aware of how you've constructed your life and the ways in which you've been seeking happiness. Having an initial reference point will allow you to more meaningfully evaluate what and how much you need to change. This increased self-awareness and self-knowledge will alone make the mindset shift to behaviors that much easier.

So, now that we're aware of what we've been doing wrong and are ready to begin concentrating on our behaviors to become and remain happy, how do we move forward from here?

The next part of the process requires us to take a closer look at the nature of behaviors and our relationship to the ones that are present in our lives.

While it might seem counterintuitive and even a little crazy, we need to agree that there is absolutely nothing in life that we "have to do" from a behavioral perspective. As we stated earlier, all of our individual behaviors are entirely within our own control. It is we, and we alone, who have complete responsibility for everything we do or don't, as our behaviors are the direct result of the decisions that each of us make. Although acknowledging this does place all of the responsibility for our lives and our happiness on us, it also gives us the power to change our own lives and ultimately allows us to become genuinely happy.

This is not to neglect the fact that things outside of our control (and as we said, most of life is inherently outside of our control) can impact us in potentially negative ways. We are just acknowledging the simple fact that, regardless of the circumstances, what we do or don't is entirely up to us. This applies equally to how we behave in response to both positive and negative experiences in our lives.

Although we've evolved as a species over the course of hundreds of thousands of years, there are some primordial aspects of our inherited nature that still profoundly influence the way many of us live our lives today.

Of these instinctual drives, fear plays perhaps the most dominant role in our lives and greatly influences the way we go about the living them. As you may have guessed, allowing fear to dominate the way we live and influence our decisions significantly inhibits our ability to become and remain genuinely happy.

As a function of our survival instinct, fear has made us fundamentally hardwired to obsessively and compulsively scan the world in front of us for threats. And even though, most of us are no longer in immediate danger of starving for lack of available food or being killed and eaten by a fellow apex predator, many of our decisions are still very much made from a place of fear. This is exactly why violence saturates modern media... because the human brain is trained to prioritize its attention on danger and threats over happiness. The presumed logic here being that as long as our basic needs are met (physical safety, food, clothing, shelter...) we'll be happy...but as we all know, this is not the necessarily the case. If it was, most of us reading this book would have no need for it in the first place and individuals who are abundantly wealthy in all material respects would always never be unhappy.

But alas, as fear is innate to the human experience and has significant influence on our behaviors, what comes to be true is that much of what we do is external-outcome driven and done purely to avoid any potentially negative consequences.

Some basic examples include:

We take out the trash so our houses don't smell badly.

We brush our teeth to prevent them from falling out.

We eat nutritious foods so that we can remain healthy.

And while we can all laugh and say, "of course we're going to do these things", it highlights the fact that there are a lot of behaviors that we consciously engage in for the primary purpose of avoiding potentially negative consequences and not because they directly support our happiness.

Just to be clear, I'm not telling you not to brush your teeth, take out the trash or binge on junk food...I'm just making a point.

The reason this is so crucial lies in the fact that we tend to apply this same logic to elements of life that extend well beyond our basic needs, and by doing so, significantly handicap our ability to manifest and sustain happiness.

If we look at things like our work or relationships, the effects of being solely motivated by fear in our decision-making and behavior become even more stark and more alarming.

How many of us work in a job that we truly dislike, but feel stuck because we have to pay bills? Similarly, how many of us remain in unhealthy or abusive relationships because we're afraid of being alone?

The primary reason why we do these and many other such things is purely to avoid what we believe to be negative consequences. We are ultimately living in, and making decisions, from a place of fear.

As a result of our inherited internal wiring and millennia of social conditioning, we've basically been primed to approach our lives and our behaviors from an inherently negative starting point.

When we view our behaviors from a negative perspective and attempt to manifest happiness with the acquisition of objects and the achievement of outcomes, what ends up happening is that we usually find ourselves being forced to increasingly engage in behaviors that do not help us manifest or sustain our happiness.

This is especially true in the modern era of hyper-materialism and hyper-consumerism, which are both fueled by egotism, insecurity, entitlement and self-centeredness. Most of us are chasing happiness through objects and outcomes, and are doing so at an ever-accelerating rate. As we continue to do this, we essentially box ourselves in to the point where all of our time and all of our resources become fully-committed and potentially over-stretched, in an effort to merely avoid the potentially negative consequences that result from this kind of chase. We no longer have the time or room to pursue that which we love and that which supports real happiness.

However, unless we're prepared to sell all of our earthly possessions and go meditate on a mountaintop for the remainder of our days, we will participate in the world, a world which is inherently a material one. There's nothing fundamentally wrong with enjoying the world around us and all that life has to offer. The problems arise when we hinge our happiness on such unreliable things.

The funny thing is, though, for all of us who have essentially allowed ourselves to become slaves and are "forced" to engage in behaviors that do not support our happiness, there are those who've gained all of the things of this world that we might want by actually engaging in behaviors that did support their happiness.

Now, these individuals may have had to do some extraordinary things or be incredibly patient for all of these worldly things to appear. However, even if that may have been the case, they had a greater likelihood of being happy all the way through the experience and not just upon the appearance of material reward.

The point being that it is not necessary to suffer in order to become happy. We are not required to do things that make us unhappy now in order to potentially become happy later. We have the power to make the decisions necessary to allow us to be happy in this very moment.

We do this by initiating a shift in our mindset towards behaviors and approaching them from a positive perspective. We engage in them solely for the sake of doing so, and because they support our happiness, and not merely to manifest objects and outcomes or avoid potentially negative consequences. We stop viewing our behaviors as merely catalysts of happiness and begin consciously recognizing what they actually are: the true source of our happiness.

It's at this point where we need to make a distinction between the two types of behaviors in which we engage.

The first is what we'll call "actualizing" behaviors, or those that ultimately support our ability to manifest and sustain happiness.

The second is what we'll call "undermining" behaviors, or those that do not ultimately support our ability to manifest and sustain happiness.

Obviously, in order to be able to manifest and sustain happiness, we want to devote as much of our time as possible to actualizing behaviors and limit the amount of time we devote to undermining behaviors.

Before we can do that, we need to figure out exactly what behaviors, of each type, are currently present in our lives.

It should be apparent that the responses to this line of questioning will be different for everyone and no one can honestly and completely answer for you. What might be good for some will be bad for others, and so long as we do not engage in behaviors that harm ourselves or anyone else, no one has the right to judge what serves as the foundation of our individual happiness.

Certainly though, not just any behaviors will suffice. We need to answer some essential questions and reflect on our answers if we want to understand what will truly serve our happiness and what will not.

The easiest way to begin is by taking an honest look at the behaviors we currently engage in (both for work and for recreation) and ask ourselves why, in fact, we engage in them. The "why" matters just as much as, if not more than, the "what".

It will be helpful to write all of this down as well because, as we alluded to earlier, it's much easier to critically think about things when they are facing us, rather than just letting them bounce around inside of our heads.

Aside from asking ourselves why exactly we engage in the behaviors that we do, we should also ask ourselves some additional questions to help sort out what behaviors are supporting our happiness and which are not.

When I engage in "X" behavior, do I...

• feel an increase or decrease in my energy levels?

• lose track of time or can't wait to be finished?

• become more attentive or more distracted?

• feel more engaged or more indifferent?

• find myself wanting to do or avoid more?

• feel passionate or apathetic?

• feel calm or irritable?

• feel the best or the worst in me is brought out?

And while you may hesitate to sit down, think about all of this and write down the things we've said it would be helpful to do so, ask yourself why you so naturally do this in the course of managing the other responsibilities in your life. Why do we fail to actively manage our own happiness in the way that we do with other important aspects of living? Do you not go see the doctor regularly for checkups? Do you not balance your checkbook every month? Do you not prioritize your tasks at work? Every single day, we devote our energy and attention to so many life responsibilities, but do we channel the same amount toward our happiness? Everything, including becoming truly happy, requires effort and there's no way around the fact that we have to do the work that is necessary if we want to make that happen.

I'm a firm believer in the lesson we can extrapolate from the emergency instructions we receive before flying on a commercial aircraft. Part of those instructions address what will happen in the event of a loss of cabin pressure...that oxygen masks will drop from the ceiling. It's the next part of those instructions that is really meaningful and applicable to the rest of our life...namely, that we should make sure to put our masks on first before even attempting to help anyone else. We cannot sufficiently take care of others if we are not ok, ourselves. This isn't selfish, it's practical and we should apply the same logic to all important aspects of our lives, including our happiness. We cannot help those around us or positively influence them if we are not genuinely happy ourselves, first.

This is why we have to actually "do the work" and devote the necessary time and energy to figuring out how to manifest and sustain happiness in our own lives. And this isn't just a one-time exercise. We must continually be vigilant about how we're living our lives and what we're devoting our time and energy toward. We also need to regularly evaluate how well we're able to manifest and sustain our own happiness.

It is essential that we live the greater part of our lives by choosing to engage in behaviors that help make us the happiest versions of ourselves, and not merely doing things as a means to an end or to avoid potentially negative consequences.

The road to happiness is marked by living in a conscious and intentional, not a reactive, way. It's effectively the difference between being purposefully driven to manifest a life of possibility and abundance by playing to "win" (becoming happy), as opposed to being motivated by fear and playing not to lose (avoiding pain).

Speedbumps and Roadblocks

Just because we're aware of an issue and have the knowledge to go about fixing it, doesn't necessarily mean that we will, or will be able to, immediately. All of us have vastly different life situations and face a variety of challenges in our lives that can cause us to move slowly or stumble on our way to becoming truly happy.

Nothing in life is linear or perpetual. We will all inevitably have to make adjustments *On The Way*.

There are some questions/challenges that you will most likely encounter as you begin to shift the focus of your happiness from objects and outcomes toward behaviors. So, let's address some of the more significant and common ones right here, right now.

"I know I'm not as happy as I could be, but I really don't know what would make me happy."

As with almost anything in life, taking the first step can be the most difficult. When we face a problem, we can become discouraged if the answer isn't right there, immediately in front of us. After all, patience isn't necessarily a modern virtue. However, we are talking about our lives and our happiness here. Nothing could be more important. Start small if you must. Big changes don't usually happen overnight and are typically the culmination of a multitude of incremental adjustments that we make over time. It's much better to be moving slowly *On The Way* to becoming happy, than to resign ourselves to a chronic state of dissatisfaction. Even the slightest adjustment in our daily lives can manifest opportunities and encounters that we had never even before imagined. Life tends to make space for the things that we devote our energy and attention toward, and it is often the case that inspiration and guidance comes in the least likely of forms and at the least likely of times. So, we need to always remain open. No matter what your life situation looks like right now, take the first step to becoming happier by identifying even the smallest of actualizing behaviors and begin engaging in it every day from this point forward. I think you'll be quickly surprised what will begin to happen once you do.

"I know I'm not as happy as I could be, but I don't have the time to go about changing my life."

Almost everything we do is done, in some way, shape or form, for the purpose of being happy. So, as we've said, if happiness is the most important thing in life, and we're not as happy as we could be, we best get to work on remedying that. In modern-day life, there are endless demands on our time, but again, everything we do or don't do is the result of a choice that we make. If you really want to do something, you'll do it, you'll make time for it. There's no such thing as "I haven't got time" when you're inspired and motivated to do something you believe to be meaningful or necessary. You have a very clear and very important choice to make here. You can continue on as you may have been, enduring the common malady of chronic dissatisfaction, or you can gather your courage and begin to make substantial and meaningful changes in your life that can potentially make you happier than you've ever been before. It's ultimately up to you.

"I know I'm not as happy as I could be, but I have other people depending on me and I have to take care of them first."

Yes, while as we said there is no such thing as a "have-to" in life and everything we do or don't is a choice, there are situations where it's best for everyone involved if another person's immediate needs are put above our own. That being said, prioritizing the needs of others before our own can become an unhealthy pattern if done so with excessive frequency. This can easily become an excuse, usually under the guise of a false sense of altruism, to not do the work of manifesting and sustaining our own happiness in order to attend to the needs of others. This happens as a result of lack of self-awareness, self-respect and/or self-motivation. As we've discussed, our happiness is our responsibility, and our responsibility alone. We owe it to ourselves to become as happy as we can possibly be (obviously without intentionally compromising the happiness of others). If we are not consistently living from a place of genuine happiness, or are not manifesting the best version of ourselves, we are not only shortchanging ourselves, we are shortchanging everyone around us, as well. The world is at its best when each individual is free to actualize their own potential and is actively engaged in doing just that.

"I know I'm not as happy as I could be, but I'm worried that if I try something different, it won't work out."

As with any endeavor, I think most of us would hope that the very first thing we try works out brilliantly. However, not only is this not typically the case, but life would be pretty boring if it were. Sometimes life needs to be slightly complicated, in a healthy way, to allow us to be challenged and grow. Just because it might take a fair amount of effort and require some "trial-and-error" along the way, there's no excuse for not beginning something potentially great just because we're afraid. Setting out *On The Way* to happiness is always going to require effort in the form of trying new and different things. As we discussed earlier, life can change, sometimes quickly and significantly. We can as well. As such, the behaviors that support our happiness today might not tomorrow and we need to not only be conscious of that fact, we have to fully accept it too. Life is game that is played, and only won by playing it well. In order to do just that, we must not only fully embrace change and all of the twists and turns that come our way, we need a few of our own. Trying new and different things is an integral part of living a happy life and should never be looked upon with fear or reluctance. We should always find excitement in the new and different, and never forget to ask ourselves, "What is the purpose of life, if not to enjoy it?".

"I know I'm not as happy as I could be, but I'm afraid of what might happen if I begin to significantly change how I live my life."

Change begets more change, so as you begin to, so will the world around you. Out of fear, we have manufactured and installed many different kinds of structures into our lives in order to give us a false sense of permanence. As we all know though, nothing is forever,...not the stars, not the rain, not the mountains and certainly not us. Acceptance of the true impermanent nature of the human experience is one of the most important things we need to do *On The Way* to becoming truly happy. Whether or not we want to become consciously aware of the fact that life situations, relationships, possessions and even ourselves are all temporary, is ultimately irrelevant, because they all are. Yes, our life situations may change. Yes, our relationships to both others and ourselves may change. Yes, we may gain or lose possessions. However, we must ground ourselves in the truth that whatever will serve us will stay, and whatever will no longer will leave. This includes everything from people to situations to possessions. Have the courage to embrace whatever supports your happiness and release whatever does not. Change, and all that comes from it, is to be celebrated, not feared.

"I know I'm not as happy as I could be and what used to support my happiness no longer seems to...now what?"

As much as we don't necessarily want to change what's seemingly worked for us in the past, we must remain conscious and aware of the moment when things start to not be working out on a consistent basis and recognize when the behaviors that used to support our happiness no longer do. The key word here is "consistent". It would be foolish to think that even *On The Way* to becoming truly happy that everything is always going to be easy and go smoothly. In fact, if everything in life starts to become too easy, that should be cause for alarm. It is more than likely that at some point we will encounter frustration with the behaviors that have supported our happiness in the past. Now, does this mean it's time for a change? Maybe, maybe not. It could just mean that we're tired or not feeling well. This is why we need to periodically evaluate to what extent the behaviors we're engaging in are supporting our happiness so that we can determine when changes actually need to be made.

"I am as happy as I could be, now how do I keep it that way?"

Lastly, it is important to note that sometimes we can become so enthusiastic and eager to engage in certain behaviors, that we become obsessive and compulsive about them. This can lead to burn out. It does not necessarily mean that a particular behavior is no longer serving us, it can just mean that we have significantly disrupted the balance in our lives. This is why it's crucial to identify a group of actualizing behaviors, or, at the very least, figure out how to engage in our behaviors in a different way to keep from becoming disinterested and unmotivated. There can be many signals that it might be time for a change, but only by remaining conscious of our relationship to everything in our lives, including our behaviors, will we truly know the answer to that.

Most of life is spent in the doing, *On The Way* there. If we're only actually "happy" when we arrive somewhere, at something, we will be happy for a relatively small amount of the time that we're alive. That is the ultimate point of sourcing our happiness with behaviors,...to be happy and enjoy our lives, in every moment.

It all comes down to the fact that you can only be the happiest, most authentic, most successful and all-around best version of yourself by engaging in the behaviors that support your happiness. When you find yourself simultaneously wholly-present and completely lost in the act of doing something that you love, greatness becomes effortless.

It doesn't ultimately matter who we want to be or what we want our lives to look like. Focusing on the behaviors that support our happiness is the only road along which anything becomes possible.

Interestingly enough, though, the longer we engage in the practice of focusing on our behaviors and de-emphasizing the importance of objects and outcomes, the way we live our lives becomes exponentially more important than what happens as a result.

As a final thought, let me leave you with this... when all is said and done, if you do what you love and love what you do, everything that you could possibly dream of (and more) will manifest in your life. By focusing on whatever it is that you love to do, without regard for what may happen as a result, you will not only find yourself *On The Way* to happiness, you will have become the living embodiment of it.

...As We Go...

So, although we've come to the end of the book, we've really come to the beginning of our journey *On The Way* toward becoming and remaining truly happy. Now that we have a better understanding of the fundamental issues that cause us to struggle with happiness, and have learned how to actually go about manifesting and sustaining it in our lives, the real work begins. True transformation only occurs when we put what we've learned into action. That's exactly what I challenge you to do, right now, today.

It would be irresponsible for me to claim, and unrealistic for you to assume, that all of your problems would be solved after finishing this book. As with anything in life, progress is a process, which is usually not linear. As I'm sure you are already aware, any significant change takes time, practice, persistence and a little patience. It isn't necessarily going to be easy, at least initially, to change your perspective on happiness and how to go about manifesting and sustaining it in your life. In fact, it's more than reasonable to expect a few setbacks here and there. Perhaps you'll occasionally slip backwards into old attitudes and patterns of behavior during periods of intense pressure or stress. That's life and we have to deal with our imperfect reality. However, we must always remember that nothing is ever actually perfected, it can only be practiced. Hopefully, no matter how many times we fall down, we end up becoming a little stronger and a little wiser every time we get back up.

Also, no matter how true or valuable a lesson or piece of wisdom might be, we need to be in the right mental, emotional and spiritual state to receive it, absorb it and live it. It is often the case that it takes time for us to fully comprehend a new idea, or at the very least, integrate it into our lives. This is one of the reasons why this book was structured in such a way that it would be relatively easy to reference as many times as you may need, going forward. I truly hope that *On The Way* will become something you will look to as you continue to grow and change.

In closing, I wish you all the very best of happiness in this life and hope that the words and ideas in this book have inspired you to become as happy as you can possibly be. There is nothing more important, and I hope by now, you've come to realize this. We are not guaranteed anything in life beyond this very moment, and as such, we should do whatever it takes to be happy right here, right now.

Made in the USA
Middletown, DE
12 April 2018